D1292754

# SNAKES SET II

# BLACK MAMBAS

Adam G. Klein
ABDO Publishing Company

# visit us at
# www.abdopub.com

Published by ABDO Publishing Company, 4940 Viking Drive, Edina, Minnesota 55435.
Copyright © 2006 by Abdo Consulting Group, Inc. International copyrights reserved in all
countries. No part of this book may be reproduced in any form without written permission from
the publisher. The Checkerboard Library™ is a trademark and logo of ABDO Publishing
Company.

Printed in the United States.

Cover Photo: Animals Animals
Interior Photos: Animals Animals pp. 7, 10, 11, 12, 17, 20; Corbis pp. 5, 6, 9, 19, 21;
    Getty Images p. 14-15

Series Coordinator: Megan Murphy
Editors: Heidi M. Dahmes, Megan Murphy
Art Direction & Maps: Neil Klinepier

## Library of Congress Cataloging-in-Publication Data

Klein, Adam G., 1976-
    Black mambas / Adam G. Klein.
       p. cm. -- (Snakes. Set II)
    ISBN 1-59679-278-7
    1. Black mamba--Juvenile literature.  I. Title.

  QL666.O64K58 2005
  597.96'4--dc22
                                                        2005042131

# CONTENTS

# BLACK MAMBAS

The black mamba is one of the deadliest animals on the planet. This **venomous** snake is found in **sub-Saharan** Africa. The name mamba comes from the **Zulu** word for "big snake."

Besides the black mamba, there are three other mamba species. Mambas belong to the Elapidae **family**, which is also called the cobra family. This is one of 11 snake families. Elapids have a pair of short, nonmoving fangs at the front of their upper jaw.

Like all snakes, mambas are reptiles. Reptiles are vertebrates, which means they have a backbone just like humans. All reptiles have scales for skin. A snake sheds its skin several times a year.

Snakes are cold-blooded creatures. They rely on outside heat sources to maintain their body temperature. Because of this, black mambas are often found **basking** on rocks or in open areas.

Black mambas have the most forward-pointing fangs of any snake. This makes their venom delivery system one of the most deadly.

# SIZES

*The black mamba is one of the most feared creatures on the African continent.*

An average adult black mamba is eight to ten feet (2 to 3 m) long. The largest one measured 14 feet (4 m). Despite their length, mambas have slender bodies. Sometimes, they are not much wider than an adult human's thumb.

The black mamba's sleek body makes it quick and agile. It can strike something that is almost half its body length away. This distance is twice as long as a typical snake can strike.

Mambas travel quickly across the ground. They carry their bodies upright, sometimes more than three feet (1 m) off the ground. The black mamba can reach speeds of seven miles per hour (11 km/h). The fastest mambas are believed to travel up to 20 miles per hour (32 km/h)!

*The black mamba's body is built for speed. Over short distances, these snakes can move faster than some humans can run!*

# COLORS

The black mamba's name is misleading. This snake is not actually black. It got its name because its mouth is inky black on the inside. When the black mamba feels threatened, it rears up. At the same time, it opens its mouth to show the dark interior.

There are a few ways to identify a black mamba in the wild. Adults are usually olive green, brown, or metallic gray. Their bellies are a lighter gray or green. Their heads are often described as being "coffin shaped."

A young black mamba is a light green color, but it darkens as it matures. Originally, this led to confusion about identifying the species. All four mamba species are green when they are young. So, the young black mambas were sometimes mistaken for green mambas.

At first glance, black mambas may appear fairly harmless. The only time people see the inside of this snake's mouth is before it attacks!

# WHERE THEY LIVE

Black mambas make their nests in **termite** mounds, animal burrows, or hollow trees. They are territorial and usually return to the same place every night. Mambas also seem to have permanent **basking** spots that they return to daily.

While primarily a **terrestrial** snake, black mambas are also at home in trees. They will often sleep on tree branches. Sometimes when they are hunting, they will travel through the trees.

*Black mambas will attack if they feel their home area is being threatened.*

*Though the black mamba is at home in trees, it spends less time off the ground than other mamba species.*

# WHERE THEY ARE FOUND

Black mambas live in south central and eastern Africa. They can be found from South Africa up the coast to Ethiopia and Sudan. They are especially concentrated in Kenya and Botswana.

*Black mambas have been known to live 12 years in captivity. They can live up to 25 years in the wild.*

Black mambas like low, open **habitats**, such as **savannas**, rocky areas, and light forests. Unlike some of their mamba cousins, they don't live in rain forests.

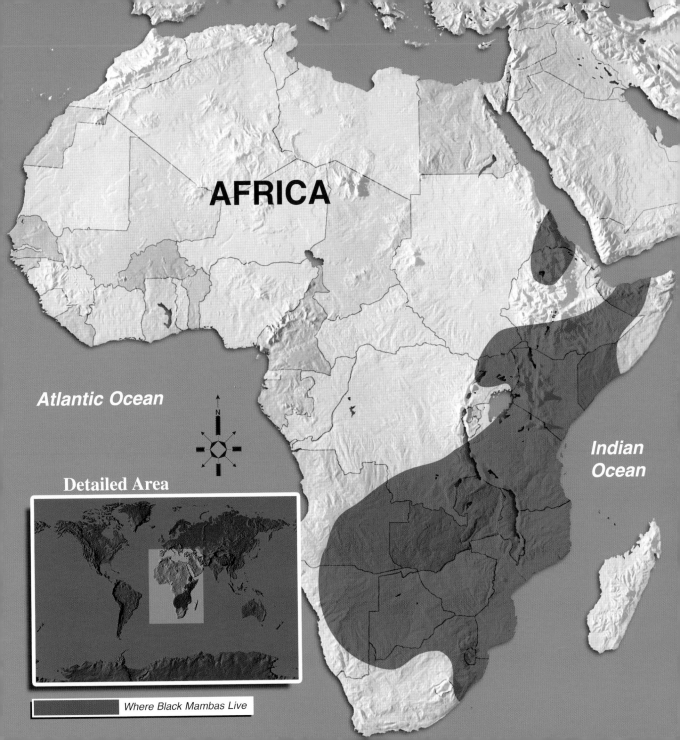

**AFRICA**

*Atlantic Ocean*

*Indian Ocean*

N

**Detailed Area**

*Where Black Mambas Live*

# SENSES

Most snakes have large, round eyes. But, they have poor vision. Snakes don't have ears either. So, they must rely on other senses to survive.

Even though snakes don't have ears, they can still sense sound. Black mambas pick up vibrations from the ground through bones in their lower jaw. This helps them find their next meal or avoid a possible **predator**.

In order to smell, the black mamba flicks out its tongue. The tongue picks up scent particles and deposits them on the roof of its mouth. There, its Jacobson's organ determines what smells are in the air. This also aids the black mamba while hunting or hiding.

A black mamba's nostrils are for breathing, not smelling. Its Jacobson's organ is what acts like a nose. This special organ is located inside the snake's mouth.

# DEFENSE

The black mamba has few natural **predators**. Mongooses and large birds are the biggest threats to its survival. Most animals fear this deadly snake.

There are many stories about mamba attacks on humans. But, black mambas are not as **aggressive** as people think. At the first sign of danger, they often go to their nests. Yet if a black mamba is cornered, it will always attack.

When a black mamba is ready to attack, it rears up and opens its black mouth. Then, it puffs out a small hood around its neck. Next, the snake makes a frightening hiss. It will strike the first thing that moves.

An adult black mamba has enough **venom** to kill five to ten adult humans. The venom causes **paralysis** and lung failure. Once a person is bitten, the venom can kill him or her in only a few hours. A bite is always fatal if left untreated. **Antivenin** is the only known treatment.

In a single bite, a black mamba can deliver ten times the amount of venom that is lethal to humans.

# FOOD

There is plenty for a black mamba to eat in **sub-Saharan** Africa. These snakes are primarily diurnal hunters. This means they hunt actively during the day. Black mambas eat squirrels and other small **rodents**. They also eat birds or even other snakes.

When hunting, the mamba strikes its prey once or twice. The **venom** is **injected** through two short, hollow fangs at the front of its mouth. After it strikes, the black mamba flees for cover.

The snake waits for the venom to take effect. The venom slowly poisons the animal's nervous system and **paralyzes** it. Its lungs stop working. Soon after the prey is dead, the snake comes out to feast.

Like other snakes, the black mamba swallows its food whole. So, the food needs to be somewhat **digested** before it reaches the stomach. The black mamba's saliva helps soften up its victim. **Enzymes** continue the absorption process. Most prey is **digested** within a few hours.

*In order to swallow its prey whole, a black mamba must first unhinge its jaw. Then, the snake can get its entire mouth around its meal.*

# BABIES

Mambas breed in spring or early summer. Several weeks after mating, the mother snake lays her eggs. Black mambas lay 6 to 17 eggs at a time.

Black mambas often choose abandoned animal burrows or **termite** mounds as nests. The eggs need to remain warm and wet. They need water and oxygen to develop. These places provide the best environment for the eggs.

*Like most snake species, mambas are more aggressive during breeding season.*

Six weeks later, the eggs hatch. Black mamba babies are born between 16 and 24 inches (41 and 61 cm) long. And, they are either a light green or gray. As they age, the snake's body will darken.

*A young black mamba may reach a length of seven feet (2 m) in its first year.*

Black mamba snakes are poisonous at birth. Even a newly hatched snake can kill a person with a proper bite. This way, a black mamba can protect itself immediately from **predators**.

The young snakes grow quickly at first. When a snake gets too big for its scales, it sheds its skin. A mature mamba sheds three to four times per year. The number of sheds depends on how often the snake eats.

# GLOSSARY

**aggressive** (uh-GREH-sihv) - displaying hostility.

**antivenin** - a kind of medicine used to reverse the effects of a poisonous snakebite.

**bask** - to lie in the heat of the sun.

**digest** - to break down food into substances small enough for the body to absorb.

**enzyme** - a complex protein produced in the living cells of all plants and animals. It is used in many of the body's functions, from digestion to clotting.

**family** - a group that scientists use to classify similar plants or animals. It ranks above a genus and below an order.

**habitat** - a place where a living thing is naturally found.

**inject** - to forcefully introduce a fluid into the body, usually with a needle or something sharp.

**paralyze** (PEHR-uh-lize) - to cause a loss of motion or feeling in a part of the body.

**predator** - an animal that kills and eats other animals.

**rodent** - any of several related animals that have large front teeth for gnawing.

**savanna** - a grassy plain with few or no trees.

**sub-Saharan** - of or relating to the part of Africa south of the Sahara desert.

**termite** - an insect that feeds primarily on wood.

**terrestrial** (tuh-REHS-tree-uhl) - living on or in the ground.

**venom** - a poison produced by some animals and insects. It usually enters a victim through a bite or sting.

**Zulu** - a tribe in Africa.

# WEB SITES

To learn more about black mambas, visit ABDO Publishing Company on the World Wide Web at **www.abdopub.com**. Web sites about these snakes are featured on our Book Links page. These links are routinely monitored and updated to provide the most current information available.

# INDEX

N

dians hold positions of responsibility in the government Indian Service, with government salaries; and tribal councils by democratic processes handle tribal interests.

Of course all is not perfect. There is still much squalor, poverty, and misery — partly due to mistakes in administering Indian lands, which are gradually being remedied. But the Indian today faces a future far brighter than any he faced in the past.

He has no problem of race prejudice. Americans, as a whole, are proud of their Indian heritage of history, customs, color, and character, and there is an abiding interest in, and admiration for, the virile red men. Whites and Indians today are friends, work together, often intermarry; throughout our history some of our greatest men have been proud of their Indian blood.

The people of the United States, having reached maturity as a nation, have found their conscience. They gave the Philippine Islands independence — and protection, even at cost of much blood. They have spent untold billions aiding war-stricken nations abroad. They have upheld the rights of weaker nations, and still do so. There are still injustices, even at home, but the great national desire of all America is to right those injustices, as soon as it can be done, whenever and wherever they occur.

So today the Indian may still dance the old dances, sing the old songs, and wear the old colorful costumes at his annual fairs and festivals. Still he may cherish the hero stories and traditions of his people.

But also he can drive and maintain tractors, bulldozers, and other machinery. He knows the secrets of irrigation and stock raising. He attends tribal meetings where speeches are made and business conducted over microphones in his own halls. He studies in schools and universities, often winning high degrees. He is adapting himself to the white man's ways, yet keeping his own. He is on the way up, looking toward a hopeful future — and still proud to be an Indian.

# INDEX

923
Wel

783

## Date Due

| | | | |
|---|---|---|---|
| SEP 23 | NOV 9 | MAY 8 | |
| SEP 30 | DEC 16 | MAY 8 | |
| OCT 8 | JAN 18 | | |
| OCT 23 | JAN 30 | SHS | |
| OCT 30 | APR 14 | AP 10 '00 | |
| NOV 13 | OCT 31 | NY 02 '00 | |
| SEP 28 | APR 6 FEB 23 | NY 15 '00 | |
| OCT 14 | DEC 3 | | |
| NOV 10 | DEC 16 | | |
| NOV 17 | APR 12 | | |
| DEC 6 | MAR 27 | | |
| JAN 20 | MAY 9 | | |
| MAY 4 | MAY 17 | | |
| SEP | OCT 6 | | |
| DEC 16 | OCT 7 | | |
| DEC 1 | APR 18 | | |
| | NOV 27 | | |

PRINTED IN U.S.A.